Will There Also Be Singing?

ALSO BY PAULETTA HANSEL

Heartbreak Tree (Madville Publishing, 2022)
Friend (Dos Madres Press, 2020)
Palindrome (Dos Madres Press, 2017)
Coal Town Photograph (Dos Madres Press, 2019)
Tangle (Dos Madres Press, 2015)
What I Did There (Dos Madres Press, 2011)
The Lives We Live in Houses (Wind Publications, 2011)
First Person (Dos Madres Press, 2007)
Divining (Woven Word Press, 2002)

Will There Also Be Singing?

poems

PAULETTA HANSEL

Shadelandhouse
MODERN PRESS

LEXINGTON, KENTUCKY

A Shadelandhouse Modern Press book
Will There Also Be Singing?
poems
Copyright © 2024, Text by Pauletta Hansel
All rights reserved.

For information about permission to reproduce selections from this book,
please direct inquiries to permissions@smpbooks.com, or
Permissions
Shadelandhouse Modern Press, LLC
P.O. Box 910913
Lexington, KY 40591

Published in the United States of America by:
Shadelandhouse Modern Press, LLC
Lexington, Kentucky
smpbooks.com
Printed in the United States of America
First edition 2024

Shadelandhouse, Shadelandhouse Modern Press,
and the logo are trademarks of
Shadelandhouse Modern Press, LLC.

ISBN: 978-1-945049-41-5
Library of Congress Control Number: 2024934921

The line *Hotcha-cha-cha-cha-cha* in the Dedication is a line
from "Appalachian Apocalypso" in Jim Webb's book,
Get In, Jesus (Wind Publications, 2013)

Cover Art:
Julyan Davis, *"A fairer maid than me?" (Young Hunting),*
oil on canvas, 50 × 46 inches
used with the artist's permission

Author photo: Owen Cramer
Cover and book design: iota book

*In loving memory of Jim Webb (1945–2018),
whose poems keep singing in the dark
Hotcha-cha-cha-cha-cha*

*In the dark times
Will there also be singing?
Yes, there will be singing.
About the dark times.*

—BERTOLT BRECHT

Contents

You Could Draw a Circle Around Where I'm From | 1

    Listen, America

    A Coal Miner's Wife Reads News of the Coronavirus

    Harlan County, USA (2019)

    Safe as Sand

    Nothing Startling

After the Plague | 4

Aerial View of Catastrophic Flooding in Eastern Kentucky | 5

No Friends of Coal | 7

A Word Like Home: A Cento | 10

Mountains | 11

My People | 12

James Hathaway Robinson:
A conversation in prose and poetry, 1919–2022 | 15

Presidents Day 2021 | 25

I Confess | 28

En/vy | 30

Drumpf | 31

November 10, 2016 | 32

On Grief: November 2016 | 33

Dis/traction | 36

washing the wounded seed: A Cento | 37

America | 38

For the Friend Who Asked Me to Write a Poem
About Breonna Taylor, 9/23/2020 | 39

Com/passion | 40

Τηε ωορλδ α σαχρεδ σπαχε
(The World a Sacred Space): A Cento | 42

Diptych | 43

Acknowledgments | 45

Author's Notes | 47

About the Author | 50

You Could Draw a Circle Around Where I'm From

> "That's where miners are getting sick.
> That's where miners are dying.
> And anybody who tells you, 'We need more information.'
> They're lying."
> *United Mine Workers President Cecil Roberts*

Listen, America

while I got air enough to speak
what you don't want to hear.
The X-rays of my lungs look like the inside
of a mountain we done mined. Scars built up
around the coal and rock dust I sucked in.
I'll need more than breath to get it out again.
Oh, lordy.
There's no one looks forward to dying.
Listen, America,
just because there ain't no more living
to be made in coal, don't mean the coal
should be taking the life out of me.

A Coal Miner's Wife Reads News of the Coronavirus

He told me, "A lot of things can get you in the mines.
They want us worrying about another fellow's
sneeze? We're used to coughing up a lung—hell, we're packed
so tight into the mantrip who can even tell whose lung it is.
I'd rather work than not." So what am I supposed to say to that?
Tell him, the paper says, *in fact last week…coal became
the most expensive fossil fuel*? A fact some wives
have known for years, but we weren't talking dollars.
Coal is so essential it's unbelievable, said the governor

who owns not just the mine but the whole damn state above it.
Unbelievable is right. I'm not one to tell my man or anybody else
to leave a job that's steady, but it's not. My husband knows it.
He's just banking on the fact he'll die while there's still work.

Harlan County, USA (2019)

Maybe it is a revelation to you,
but miners know how to stop a train.
Maybe you think that love of coal
means love of the company.
Let me tell you what we love
about coal.
It's the paycheck.
The one we don't have.
It's the food
that's not on the table,
the new backpack
that won't be on his back
my boy's first day of school.
The doctor his granny
won't be seeing for her heart.
Remember, we're used to the dark.
We can see the car on the track
filling up in the mine
you pulled us out of.
We can see inside your pockets
lined green from the rock we dug for free.

Safe as Sand

Was it dusty?
Lord, yes.
We'd drive our trucks through glittered clouds.
But no need to worry; you could eat a pound a day,
they told us. No masks either.
 It would look bad for tourists headed out to the lake.
Most days we'd laugh it away. Coal ash flu.
Our skin flaked off like fish scales.
Of course, they knew.
I never saw one of them sucking in the dust.
But workers? We were birds blown out of the mine.
They tested the fish for arsenic.
Not us. We made a shrine up by the plant for those already dead
from the cancer—liver, brain, leukemia. My wife,
she lays a penny there, says this is more than what we're worth
to those who own this Tennessee Valley.

Nothing Startling

When it comes to the mining company and
it comes to the worker, production is all there
is. It's all there ever was.
How much dust I suck in? How long I'm going to live? Nothing.
Someone else is there to take my place. There's no startling
the rock from my lungs. No finding the heart in
the company. There's no cut long enough to reach the
seam. You want something to change, you might try to change the weather.

After the Plague

Cicadas are not locusts,
though their apocalyptic
scream proclaims not lust
to me. Another deadly.
Wrath rains down
in decibels. My fear
projected on this world.

Aerial View of Catastrophic Flooding in Eastern Kentucky

Quicksand, Bulan, Neon, Hiner, Martin, Fisty.
This is our place in Hueysville.
This was my Mother's house before she passed.
Samantha's sister's house is by that blue bridge.
Anyone know anything about Fugate's Fork Road?
Stringtown, Ajax, Isom, Pinetop, Dwarf.
This is my cousin's house.
My Mamaw's house is on the left.
That bridge is about 8 feet above
where the creek's supposed to be.
Isn't this Mary's house?
This is the mouth of our hollow,
the red arrow was our road in.
Nix Branch, Jakes Branch, Trot.
If you zoom in to where the white car hood is,
my home is there.
Rowdy, Wayland, Noble's Landing, Cowan Creek.
OMG that is Pigeon Roost.
Hindman, Buckhorn, Chavis, Krypton, Garrett,
over toward Pound.
Y'all this is my hometown.
This little tree, and God, kept us alive this morning.
My daughter swam with her dog to a neighboring rooftop.
Does anyone know about Kite, KY?
Caney, Possum, Ary, Lost Creek, Hardburly, Trace.
Dad and my nephew are neck deep
they need help
please.
Are you all safe??
We lost the farm animals and 5 cats.
Lost my chainsaws so I can't even work.
You need to understand the nature of the topography.

Add to that strip mining, climate change, political neglect.
We have lost everything
again.
We have warm beds, clothes, and toiletries available.
We have hot showers and food.
Anyone trapped in downtown Whitesburg is welcome to come.
We need help and I'm willing to help anyone
in the same shape we are.
Your prayers are good
but we need to get federal and state assistance ASAP.
Don't cry for Appalachia, work for change however you can!
Let's use the internet to tell our story.
Thank you for posting.
Much love and many blessings to you all
from what's left.

No Friends of Coal

> "What a Friend we have in Jesus, / All our sins and griefs to bear!"
> *Traditional hymn.*

> "And he shall break down the house, its stones and timber and all the plaster of the house, and he shall carry them out of the city to an unclean place."
> *Leviticus 14:45*

And when the unclean place
is the silt pond
up by the strip mine and the gray
of its waters broke free
from its rickety dam
and carried away your house built
wise as you could, what else but a lawsuit
to carry the blame
back up the shorn mountain
where it belongs?

"What a friend we have in…"

Jesus wept
and I'm willing to wager he would again
at Blackhawk Coal and their claims
of "our people" and "deeply impacted,"
their sympathies and their support.
And the mud had not dried
when they posted their notice
"Intent To Blast"
over where the door stoop had been
before the flood.

I know there was rain,
too much, too fast,
another one of those 1000-year floods,
but what kind of flood
carries its little ashy silt pond fishes
down from what's left of the mountain,
not up from the creek?

> "Within minutes of the color change, the water rose so high
> that it picked up homes, cars, sheds, boulders, trees,
> staircases, swing sets and swimming pools."

"No Friends of Coal"
reads the headline about the lawsuit
in the local weekly paper
underneath the photo of what used to be
that young man's house,
now torn down to its timbers,
its moldy plaster spread out on the stony ground,
the raptors circling just beyond the frame.

> "And the Philistine said to David, Come to me,
> and I will give thy flesh unto the fowls of the air,
> and to the beasts of the field." 1 Samuel 17:44

That young man's name is not David.
I wish he were David, delivered
"out of the paw of the lion,
 and out of the paw of the bear,"
and "out of the hand of this Philistine."

So, yes, I'm feeling biblical,
Old and New,
calling on Jesus
to back up his people,
once clothed and fed by coal.
The ones who lost everything
there on Lost Creek, along River Caney.
The ones that are fixing to lose
every friend they thought they had.

    "What a friend we have in…"

Brother, I am here to tell you,
no matter the money they used to pay,
you don't have a friend in coal.

A Word Like Home: A Cento

Alone on a ridge,
barbed wire nailed to rotting posts—
can you feel the ghosts in your chest
disappear into the swirl
of early spring? The first light
faded into the rough patina of oil stains, and long-dead
gardens wait at the top of farms,
holler lined with beech, oak, willow—verdant skeletons.
I try to believe the river lives in the body,
just a variant of blue before night folds in with scraps of stars,
knowing what those who follow earth's pull know.
Like the spine of a sleeping panther,
my mother tongue unrolls.
Name the hills and what they tell you of yourself.
Our stories are ferried in its depth: caravan of arrowhead, latchkey, crockery, bone.
Peepers in the pond singing their own song,
quivering a different kind of arrow, the piercing shaft of arcing voice
remembering where the world ends and home begins.
Something shakes the trees and a hundred or a thousand miles away their children turn as one
to scream a word like home
under pine sighs, near the stony mumble of
visiting spirits of those we once loved and lost.
What would it take to remember where you come from?
Except today you are driving and listening to
years of homely music: the tinny gripe of the
zenith radio: Bill Anderson is singing like country music is God's voice. Nothing more,
    nothing less.

Mountains

I would have said that I despised them, had anybody asked.
More true to say I saw them only in their absence,

there along the northbound road where green becomes
a shallow bowl of sky, and I could breathe again.

I would have said that, I *can breathe again,*
the sort of sentence I composed inside my head.

One-sided dialogue in the ongoing screenplay of my life
with words like *pensive, intellectual, art,* not words

that lend themselves to towns notched in the hollows
between hills. A sort of sepia wash, coal dust spit out

from the trucks. I would have said that too, had I turned
my eye beyond the movie of the girl who's going someplace

else. And so when I get myself somewhere, at last, small
city teetering on a river's rim, and drive each morning

to a job, three-story walk-up tucked in the shadow
of the land's slight rise—surprise to feel the ache of home.

My People

Once I'd see those not-quite city
houses tucked between river
and road or up a gravel lane,
place for a garden, two cars for parts,
and think—my people.
My vowels would slow and stretch
a hand to theirs. Now
I scan for other signs—
MAGA, Trump, the battle lines
scored scars crisscrossed against
illusion of who and what was ever mine.

James Hathaway Robinson:
A conversation in prose and poetry, 1919–2022

James Hathaway Robinson, Sr. was born in Sharpsburg, Kentucky, the son of Nathaniel and Martha Robinson. He moved to Cincinnati, Ohio in 1915 to teach sixth grade at the Douglass School.... He was also author of a number of publications, including the "Cincinnati Negro Survey" (later called "The Negro in Cincinnati"), published by the National Conference of Social Work in 1919.
—Notable Kentucky African Americans Database

[After World War II, the economic] push and pull model of migration left millions of Appalachians displaced from their homes and created a new Urban Appalachian diaspora. As ... migrants formed substantial communities in urban areas like Cincinnati, the existing neighborhoods they moved into responded negatively to their presumed deficits, terming their presence the "SAM (southern Appalachian migrant) problem."
— Urban Appalachian Community Coalition Website

When a white woman from Appalachia

        "Then came the influx or hordes from the South,
        white and colored, the one usually hostile…

chooses to write a poem about a black man from Appalachia

        "and the other too often the less progressive type…

called up to Cincinnati to investigate "the Negro problem"
is she looking for herself?

> "Conditions in the city went from bad to worse."
> James Hathaway Robinson, 1919

My people, his people…

> "The Negro lives by himself, works by himself"
> suffers sick "by himself in the colored ward…

Unlike me, Robinson had no illusions

> "[And] when he dies, "he is buried by himself whether in a colored cemetery or the colored section of the Potter's Field."

that our people were one and the same.

> "The presumption is invariable against the Negro and he is often arrested and sentenced where others. ….

I am the other.

> 'would be excused. [And the press gives] undue publicity to [black] weaknesses, foibles and crimes, while seldom mentioning black accomplishments and virtues…

We want to believe things are different now.

> "because they lack news value."

When I moved up to Cincinnati in 1979,
I didn't know there were neighborhoods
where I wasn't supposed to live.
I was proud of this.

>In addition, he reported the "almost universal" tendency…

Integration or gentrification?

>to charge black tenants higher rents.

My ignorance is inexcusable.

>[Robinson] outlined specific economic causes in the South [for the migration… of southern blacks to the North]—low wages, high prices, "the disadvantages of the crop-lien system," flood destruction, and the boll weevil.

While we may now add to the list,
boom-and-bust industry
and the automation of the coal mines,

>Out of 40 migrants, 27 said they had come North for better wages, 6 for "better privileges," 5 "to better condition," 2 because of "bad treatment" in the South, and 1 "just took a notion."

I will admit that the notion of my leaving Appalachia

>In his presentation Robinson characterized Cincinnati as "a northern city with a southern exposure, a gateway between North and South used alike by fugitive slave and freeman of yesterday and migrant of today in their quest of Utopia…"

is one I can't remember living without.

> To the black, he said, Utopia is a place "where a man is a man," a place that is "seemingly a much sought after but ever fleeting if ever existing Land of Nowhere."

Not then.
Not now.

> "Not only do hotels, restaurants and soda fountains refuse to serve him, but moving picture houses and private parks refuse to admit him; theaters segregate and often embarrass him."

But God bless the child who's got his own.
Right?

> The black business community was not large, and, he found, it tended to be dominated by the small shops run by such entrepreneurs as undertakers, barbers, tailors, cobblers, beauticians, …

Until he doesn't.
May I remind you of the West End,

> druggists, insurance men, grocers, caterers, newspaper editors, real estate agents, printers….

a little after Robinson's time,
barely before my own?

> The professional class, on the other hand was "of considerable numbers" and included doctors, dentists, lawyers, ministers. teachers, and social workers…"

In 1958, 25,737 people lived in the section of the West End
that is now called Queensgate,

                          Even among this more successful group, however,
                          Robinson pointed out that "various handicaps
                          prevent the development of men of wide
                          reputations."

about the same population of today's
Oakley, Hyde Park, and East Walnut Hills neighborhoods combined.
Progress or displacement.
I won't honor that with a question mark.

                          Robinson called for self-origination of group
                          consciousness …

In 2006, over 25 years after I moved to Cincinnati,
my husband and I bought a house in Paddock Hills,

                          among the city's black people.…

Cincinnati's "best-kept secret,"
according to our community website.

                          and for a campaign of education

Built in the 1920s, and settled first by Catholics and then by Jews,

                          among white people.

the first black families moved to the area in 1966,

                          Racial discrimination, Robinson thought, was
                          based in white people's ignorance of black life, …

and, according to that website
"Paddock Hills was racially balanced by 1975

                      [knowing] little of his "aspirations, handicaps, disappointments."

"and has successfully maintained integration ever since."

                      [In 1919] at the main entrance to the Douglass School, [the only remaining all-black public school left in Cincinnati from the nineteenth-century "Colored School" system],…"four huge placards confront the visitor."

In 2006, each corner of our yard
abutted yards where black people lived.

                      These proclaimed the following slogans:
                      "Self-Control; …

In the last ten years,

                      "Self-Reliance;…

by my informal and unscientific count

                      "Self-Respect;,,,

white has replaced black in almost every real estate transaction.

                      "and Race Pride!"

Integration?

[Robinson's] hope for ... the African American people lay in organizing the institutions that served the community into a coherent whole, ...

or disintegration?

and organizing among individuals a sense of belonging to a community.

"Our Black Lives Matter signs staked in yards
where black children once played."
Pauletta Hansel, 2021

But Robinson did not describe what had attracted him to the Queen City, a town with "a southern racial relationship."

Presidents Day 2021

I.
Friend, I can't stop thinking about race,
today, and by race, I mean whiteness,
mine and yours, and if I am honest (I am trying
to be honest), that of almost everyone
I know. This neighborhood is getting whiter,
and I'm not talking about the February snow
that coats our cars and lawns and sidewalks.
Fifteen years ago, we were the nice white couple
next door, across the street, backyard abutting yard.
Now there's too many of us for me to count.
Our Black Lives Matter signs are staked in lawns
where black children played.
My husband's children called these tree-lined cul-de-sacs
the ghetto.
I'd like to say we moved here, then,
to give his suburban teens a better view.
In truth, we moved here for those trees, this house, the yard,
the picture of the kind of whiteness
we might learn to be. But mixed neighborhoods
don't mean we don't still sort ourselves by color,
like to like.

II.
Today I walk the snow-packed streets, composing
in my mind these lines
I'll write to you.
I am careful where I put my foot. This whiteness
covers ice and cracks I cannot see.
The scarf that's wrapped around my neck—
gold-flecked black against the cardinal red

of my down coat—was given to me
by black women I love. Their hands
eased my mother's pain; their faces
ease my memory of her years of dying.
We hold her close by keeping each other near.
And still, we are so careful.
We watch where we step.

III.

Do you remember where you were 2008,
Election Day, Barack Obama?
Of course, you do.
In this room where I now write, I watched
his victory speech recorded on the internet,
Michelle dressed in red on black, starlight beside him.
I cheered my silent cheers while my stepdaughter slept.
I'd taken her to see some fluff of white girls
whining on the movie screen. I tried
to fill and smooth the cracks between us, then.
Now she bemoans all the ways her family
raised her to be racist.
As we did.
As we all were raised,
we who are white.

IV.

I know I told you of my father's march for justice,
Main Street, Richmond, Kentucky, May 1961.
White stones thrown against our house.
I probably never shared the story my parents told me,
how at five-years-old I'd tried to talk away their tears

during Walter Cronkite, 1965, the bloody march
from Selma to Montgomery:
"It's okay," I told them,
"They're only black."

V.
I wear my whiteness lightly,
like a down-filled coat. I hardly know
it's there, unless I'm called out to the cold
without it. And, friend, how often am I
called to that?

I Confess

These days I think too much
about assassination, and let me just say
I have come down against it every time,
swatting it away, a plague-ridden fly

in my otherwise mild and law-abiding imagination,
and I do not accept the legal argument
that targeted killings are a country's form
of self-defense, regardless of whether the target

will ever see the inside of a detention center,
and be faced with deciding, like thousands
of seven-year-olds, should the assigned Mylar blanket
go over or under on the mud-caked concrete floor.

Every time, I rise up on the right side of the question
though I have gone so far as to research the word
from the Arabic, *hashshashin*, the Assassins of Persia,
perhaps so-named for the necessity of getting high

before slipping in the blade. (In private,
some Border Patrol agents consider migrant deaths
a laughing matter; others are succumbing to depression,
anxiety, or substance abuse.)

How, with or without the name, the act
is older than our ability to write it down.
How way back in the Old Testament,
there it was alongside the begetting and begats.

How in the Roman Empire, strangling in the bathtub
was the method of choice for murdering one's king,
while, as you might expect, in Japan it was the sword.
Here in the US we, as always,

prefer the gun, and let me just say,
I do not and will not own one.
I confess only to the image in my mind
of the mongrel dogs of history lapping at the wound.

En/vy

The Old French,
        how well they understood
the danger
        of outside looking in:
                videre from *weid*, "to see,"
        at the green root
of all wisdom
        and wit, invidious or otherwise,
of twit   and video,
        our kaleidoscopic view.

One of   the seven
        deadlies,
            the ten
        shall nots.

Dante's purgatorial eyes
wired shut.

Cain over Abel,
        the Towers of Babel
                and Trump—only pride
more weights the soul.

The evil eye is cast,
        uneasy,
from the head
that wears the crown.

Drumpf

You live in rented rooms,
Mr. President, nothing
belongs to you, not
my ragged country, not
my worn body
you would sell cheap
for parts, not
even your
name.

November 10, 2016

Today in Orange County, Florida
a bald eagle got trapped
in a storm drain.
What I know about
Florida or eagles
could fit on the tip of this pen
(and never would I have thought
them together on the page)
but I do know something
about metaphor when it
wings up to flap in my face,
and that something is flailing
flightless, with talons,
on the breath of a country—
mine—
suspended.
I am waiting
for the worst that can happen.
I'm afraid
we've seen nothing yet.

On Grief: November 2016

I.
The 6th stage of grief
is *meaning*, says the man
who ought to know, the one
up at the death and dying podium
who flies around the country
fueled by our tears.
I like this guy.
He says no matter how rich
the meaning, it is
never worth the cost.
But we're a meaning-making animal,
(that's me talking now) always
searching for some reason,
as if this unnatural
disaster of a president-elect
will turn out to be
the push-to-the-cliff-edge
this country needed, or maybe
its's how Mary meets Bob, or Barb
or Miguel at the No Trump March
and the kid they'll raise
will cure dementia
someday, but too late
for my mother,
or Ronald Reagan
or our country,
and maybe for me,
if Mom has the kind
that runs in the family,
after all.

II.
Back at the nursing home,
the shriveled lady whose dementia
is resting step or two
before my mom's
looks over the table at us
as my fingers slip some bits of fruit
between my mother's lips
and asks, *Who has your heart?*
I'd say it's pretty obvious, which maybe
is her point, or maybe not. My mother
doesn't have my heart, not literally,
but I read on the internet
(therefore it must be true)
that fetal cells remain
inside the mother's body
all her life, and so she may
have me in her heart,
or in her spleen,
or a bit of me floating around
her withering brain,
which might explain
how she can tell me, sometimes,
what I had for dinner,
or who just died, or that the apples
we bought from the market
aren't worth the cost.

III.
The principles of grief work,
the grief guy declares,
are say goodbye
to who they were, start new
with whoever they are now.
And my mother and I
are doing pretty well,
at least today,
with our comingling cells
but I don't think
I will be making nice
with the country we're about to get.
It's Bedtime for Bonzo
all over again,
except without directors
or a script
and the contract on America
has been renewed,
this time as unreality television.
The last TV show I really liked
was Buffy the Vampire Slayer
from way back when the other
Clinton was in office. I know
I'm not the only one;
just last week I saw a rusting Toyota
with the bumper sticker,
What Would Buffy Do?
She'd kick some ass,
that's what. I'm going to
stick with anger,
stage two.

Dis/traction

Drawn asunder,

                      dragged,

as

      by tractor,

"a poor mad soul," so driven   /   or split,

      as in

           "I was

                of three

                      minds, like a tree in which"

                there's an iPhone,

          a book, and down below, my

     body, rooted still in good

dirt.

washing the wounded seed: A Cento

I.

back in the days when no one refused to sing
when politics was an argument among friends
may you be counted among the fortunate/though the state
might hope for clear/specific steps/whip
thumb & index/this is now your prayer
the necessary art of ignoring it as it curdles
we can no longer speak

II.

the seed must be strong enough
you might expect a pinch of pluck/of backbone
of lack & want/will it return twofold/threefold
I sent my roots up into the atmosphere
to/cleanse/
you back from death/weep you present
do not think
each disappeared

III.

to those gathered/present/I ask
are you still here?/and do you
hear the echo to guide me/find
his song/to the song/sung by his father
read & savor them/recite & chant them
speaking the truest truth

America

America, I am not singing you
beautiful. I do not hear the melody beneath the roiling
clang and clatter of your
discord. I did not know I loved you, America,
even broken as you were, until the
fist came down. *Don't it always seem to
go, you don't know what you* thought you
had until the dream of it
is gone.
Jolted awake, I sing your name, *Ameri-
ka*, a stumbling, tired
lament, a hum beneath my breath in
minor key. A lone
note dirge.
One word—
Please—
quavering syllable to
raise you up. I cannot
sing you to your grave.
This land is my only home, America,
unsound in its frame. You are deaf now, to our
varied carols sung across your shorn mountains, above your
withered plains. I am
exiled, America, even as I walk
your streets, singing
Zion, we lay down and wept, and wept, for thee.

For the Friend Who Asked Me to Write a Poem About Breonna Taylor, 9/23/2020

Because she said today the only words
she had to say were ugly.
Because injustice is a dark shot
that always hits its mark.
Because a knee on the neck
of a dying man
has lost all metaphorical possibility.
Because a sleeping woman cannot say,
"They'll kill me. They'll kill me."
Because they did.
Because they will again.
Because I live with the luxury of breath
I give this breath to say their names
more beautiful than any words of mine:
Natasha
Janisha
Meagan
Maya
Sandra
India
Betty
Korryn,
Deborah
Charleena
Atatiana
Breonna

Com/passion

Loaned across the languages,
to Latin   from Greek to
       com "I am with you" and
       passio, "I suffer,"
of the kind that is kin
to adoration and Christ
on a cross and suffer little children
to come unto…   *Pati,* the same root
    as in patience and
        patients,

the acronym, PATI:
    Penetrating Abdominal Trauma Index;
        Public Access to Information—
too much information
leads to compassion fatigue.
   "The near enemy"
of compassion is sorrow, is pity, is
    handwringing,
        ass sitting,
            woe unto-ing
every last one of us:

    the "pathological empathy of our age"
is compatible with Twitter
and Facebook and "idiot compassion,"
the general tendency to give people what they…
      ♪ … can't always get … ♪
because you can't stand with their suffering
long enough
      to be what they need.

What you need.

What I need…

    "A heart
    broken open
    like a geode to the rare space within,"
says *Roshi* Joan Halifax.

I am with you, buddy,
        (*Buddy*: mid-19th century; perhaps an alteration of brother, as in,
        "can you spare…?")

my heart on permanent loan.

Τηε ωορλδ α σαχρεδ σπαχε
(The World a Sacred Space): A Cento

a blood moon tonight &
licks of flame, fallen stars,
the ones from the mouths
of our ancestors,
a question I couldn't answer.
Yet my bones sing
in the space between.
Imagine your electric heart
pressed into that whorl
of ruby moon hyacinth.
A man boards a train
going somewhere.
Spider respins a broken web.
Moon walks in her sleep.
This splintered world,
the only one that matters.

Diptych

Two does not mean torn.
Not always. The child

gazes at his fingers, as if
they hold the questions.

The mother's eyes
look out toward dark.

Patchwork of red bleeds
into gold. Sunrise or set.

You must create
the other side yourself.

Before. The not-yet-mother,
nimbus cloud awaits the rain.

Or after. The stone rolled
to or from the tomb.

There is a hinge. Close
the two sides together

and you have a book. It is
an old story. How it's told

depends on how
you open it again.

Acknowledgments

Many thanks to the editors of the following print and online publications who published these poems, some in previous form:

Cutleaf (January 2022)
"En/vy"

Heartbreak Tree (Madville Publishing, 2022)
"I Confess" (First print publication)

LexPoMo.com
"My People" (2022)
"After the Plague" (2021)
"washing the wounded seed" (2018)
"Τηε ωορλδ α σαχρεδ σπαχε (The World a Sacred Space): A Cento" (2022)

NewVerse News
"Aerial View of Catastrophic Flooding in Eastern Kentucky" (August 2, 2022)
"No Friends of Coal" (September 6, 2022)

Northern Appalachian Review
"You Could Draw a Circle Around Where I'm From" (Vol. 2, 2021)
"Listen, America" (Vol. 2, 2021)
"A Coal Miner's Wife Reads News of the Coronavirus" (Vol. 2, 2021)
"Nothing Startling" (Vol. 1, 2020)

Pine Mountain Sand & Gravel
"Safe as Sand" (Vol. 24, 2021)
"Presidents Day 2021" (Vol. 21, 2018)
"America" (Vol. 21, 2018)

Pudding Magazine #70, 2021
"A Coal Miner's Wife Reads News of the Coronavirus"

Race and the City — Art, curator, Saad Ghosn (Ghosn Publishing, 2023)
"James Hathaway Robinson: A conversation in prose and poetry, 1919–2022"

Rattle: Poets Respond
"I Confess" (July 7, 2019)
"Harlan County, USA 2019" (Aug. 14, 2019)

Troublesome Rising: A Thousand-Year Flood in Eastern Kentucky, ed. Melissa Helton (Fireside Industries, University of Kentucky Press, 2024)
First print publication of:
"Aerial View of Catastrophic Flooding in Eastern Kentucky"
"No Friends of Coal"

Undocumented: Great Lakes Poets Laureate on Social Justice, ed. Ronald Riekki and Andrea Scarpino (Michigan State University Press, 2019)
"On Grief: November 2016"
"November 10, 2016"

What Things Cost: an anthology for the people, eds. Rebecca Gayle Howell, Ashley M. Jones, and Emily J. Jalloul (University of Kentucky Press, 2023)
"I Confess"

Women Speak Anthology, Vol. 9 (Women of Appalachia Project's 15th Anniversary Edition), ed. Kari Gunter-Seymour (Sheila-Na-Gig, 2024)
"Dis/traction"
"For the Friend Who Asked Me to Write a Poem About Breonna Taylor, 9/23/2020
Com/passion"

Author's Notes

You Could Draw a Circle Around Where I'm From
This found poem was spoken by United Mine Workers President Cecil Roberts at the West Virginia Black Lung Association conference in June 2019, as reported in:
>Boles, Sydney. *Ohio Valley ReSource*. "As Calls For Action On Black Lung Disease Grow, Regulators Show Little Indication Of Change." WOUB Public Media. June 8, 2019. https://woub.org/2019/06/08/as-calls-for-action-on-black-lung-disease-grow-regulators-show-little-indication-of-change/.

Listen, America
The poem includes quotes from interviews in:
>Peterson, Erica, and Benny Becker. *Ohio Valley ReSource*. "Living With Black Lung: Coal Miners Caught In A Surging Epidemic." Louisville Public Media. February 12, 2018. https://ohiovalleyresource.org/2018/02/09/living-with-black-lung-coal-miners-caught-in-a-surging-epidemic/.

A Coal Miner's Wife Reads News of the Coronavirus
This was drafted in the spirit of a golden shovel, using words from the line "They used to work in a coal mine. Not steady work…," in Muriel Rukeyser's 1938 *The Book of the Dead*, reprinted by West Virginia University Press in 2018. Italicized lines from:
>Englund, Will. "Coal miners told to keep working during the outbreak despite close quarters, damaged lungs." *The Washington Post*. March 24, 2020. https://www.washingtonpost.com/business/2020/03/24/coal-miners-coronavirus/.

Harlan County, USA (2019)
Some phrases are from quotes in:
>James, Connor, and Will Puckett. "'No pay, we stay'; Protesting miners in Harlan County are not going anywhere." Mountain News WYMT. July 29, 2019. https://www.wymt.com/content/news/Unpaid-miners-want-answers-as-train-carries-coal-away-from--513348141.html.

The mine from which the coal is blocked from leaving belongs to Revelation Energy LLC, which filed for Chapter 11 bankruptcy protection on July 1, 2019, along with its affiliate Blackjewel LLC.

Safe as Sand
This was drafted in the spirit of a golden shovel, using words from the lines "No masks. / Most of them were not from this valley…," in Muriel Rukeyser's 1938 *The Book of the Dead*, reprinted by West Virginia University Press in 2018. The poem also includes material from the following news sources:
>Loller, Travis. Associated Press. "Sick and dying workers demand help after cleaning coal ash." *The Spokesman-Review*. August 28, 2019. https://www.spokesman.com/stories/2019/aug/28/sick-and-dying-workers-demand-help-after-cleaning-/.
>
>Bourne, Joel K., Jr. "Coal's other dark side: Toxic ash that can poison water and people." *National Geographic*. February 19, 2019. https://www.nationalgeographic.com/environment/article/coal-other-dark-side-toxic-ash.

Nothing Startling
This is a golden shovel using a line from the Gwendolyn Brooks poem "The White Troops Had Their Orders but the Negroes Looked Like Men" in:
>Brooks, Gwendolyn. *Selected Poems*. New York: Harper & Row, 1963.

It includes words spoken by former miner Harold Sturgill at the West Virginia Black Lung Association conference in June 2019, as reported in:
>Boles, Sydney. *Ohio Valley ReSource*. "As Calls For Action On Black Lung Disease Grow, Regulators Show Little Indication Of Change." WOUB Public Media. June 8, 2019. https://woub.org/2019/06/08/as-calls-for-action-on-black-lung-disease-grow-regulators-show-little-indication-of-change/.

Aerial View of Catastrophic Flooding in Eastern Kentucky
This poem composed of excerpts from Facebook posts on July 28, 2022.

No Friends of Coal
The title of this poem is from an August 24, 2022, headline in *The Jackson Times-Voice*. The poem draws on national news coverage for many of its details:
>McCausland, Phil. "One flood-ravaged Kentucky community is suing a coal company, saying its negligence made damage even worse." NBC News. August 22, 2022. https://www.nbcnews.com/news/us-news/one-flood-ravaged-kentucky-community-suing-coal-company-saying-neglige-rcna43532.

A Word Like Home: A Cento
This is an abecedarian cento composed of lines from poems in:
>Gunter-Seymour, Kari, ed. *I Thought I Heard a Cardinal Sing: Ohio's Appalachian Voices*. Sheila-Na-Gig Editions, 2022.

Lines are from the following poets, in this order: Michael Rainwater, Jennifer Hambrick, Teagan Hughes, Sylvia Freeman, Myrna Stone, Phoebe Reeves, Sherrell Wigal, Colby Smith, Abby Wheeler, KB Ballentine, Penelope Moffet, Mark Jordan, Donna Hilbert, Marjorie Maddox, Barbara Sabol, Kristine Williams, Mark Jordan, Michael Rainwater, Steve Abbott, Sean Kelbley (also the title), Richard Hague, Robert DeMott, Matthew Gilbert, Kristine Williams, and Roy Bentley.

James Hathaway Robinson: A conversation in prose and poetry, 1919–2022
The piece is meant to be read in two voices—the left margin and the right indent. After the headnotes, all indented passages are taken directly or closely paraphrased from "James Hathaway Robinson and the Origins of Professional Social Work in the Black Community," by Andrea Tuttle Kornbluh, in:
>Taylor, Henry Louis, Jr., ed. *Race and the City: Work, Community, and Protest in Cincinnati, 1820–1970*. Illinois: University of Illinois Press, 1993.

Quotation marks are used only when Kornbluh is quoting others. Many of Robinson's quotes come from the "Cincinnati Negro Survey" (later called "The Negro in Cincinnati"), published by the National Conference of Social Work in 1919. Additional external sources include: "God Bless the Child," by Billie Holiday and Arthur Herzog Jr.; "25,737 People Lived in Kenyon-Barr When the City Razed It to the Ground," by Alyssa Konermann in *Cincinnati Magazine*; the Paddock Hills community website; my essay on Union Terminal/Queensgate, first published in Belt Publishing's *Cincinnati Neighborhood Guidebook*; and my poem "President's Day, 2021."

I Confess
The parenthetical is from:
> Raff, Jeremy. "What a Pediatrician Saw Inside a Border Patrol Warehouse." *The Atlantic*. July 3, 2019. https://www.theatlantic.com/politics/archive/2019/07/border-patrols-oversight-sick-migrant-children/593224/.

Drumpf
The German surname that is likely predecessor to that of the 45th president of the United States.

November 10, 2016
This poem was inspired by:
> Chan, Melissa. "Bald Eagles Trapped in Florida Sewer Drain Draw Comparisons to Current State of America." TIME. November 10, 2016. https://time.com/4567367/bald-eagles-florida-orlando-sewer/.

On Grief: November 2016
"The man who ought to know" is David Kessler.

Dis/traction
This poem includes a line from "Thirteen Ways of Looking at a Blackbird" by Wallace Stevens and a nod to Shakespeare.

washing the wounded seed: A Cento
This poem is composed of lines from each poem in Jeremy Paden's *Prison Recipes* (Broadstone Books, 2018), a book dedicated to the victims of Argentina's state-sponsored violence, often called the Dirty War. This new poem holds my own country in its heart.

America
This poem includes phrases from the songs "Big Yellow Taxi," "This Land is Your Land" and "By The Waters Of Babylon" and from Walt Whitman's "I Hear America Singing."

For the Friend Who Asked Me to Write a Poem About Breonna Taylor, 9/23/2020
This poem includes a partial list of African American women killed by police. Lonormi Manuel is the friend who requested the poem.

Com/passion
This poem includes a quote from Roshi Joan Halifax's book *Standing at the Edge* (Flatiron Books, 2018).

Τηε ωορλδ α σαχρεδ σπαχε (The World a Sacred Space): A Cento
This poem is composed of lines from poems published on lexpomo.com (2022) by Liz Prather (also the title), Kevin Nance, Karen George, Tabitha Dial, Gaby Bedetti, Melva Sue Priddy, Alissa Sammarco, Jennifer Beckett, Pam Campbell, Jim Lally, Linda Bryant, and Nancy Jentsch.

About the Author

Pauletta Hansel's ten poetry collections include *Will There Also Be Singing?*, *Heartbreak Tree*, which won the Poetry Society of Virginia's 2023 Poetry Book Award for North American Writers and Publishers, and *Palindrome*, winner of the 2017 Weatherford Award for Appalachian poetry. Her first book, *Divining*, led to Hansel being named 2002 Ohio Poet of the Year. She was born and raised in southeastern Kentucky. Her writing is featured in *Oxford American*, *Rattle*, *Poetry Daily*, *Appalachian Review*, *Appalachian Journal*, and *Still: The Journal*, among others. Hansel was the 2022 Writer-in-Residence for The Public Library of Cincinnati and Hamilton County, previously having served as Cincinnati's first Poet Laureate. She is past managing editor of *Pine Mountain Sand & Gravel*, the literary publication of Southern Appalachian Writers Cooperative, and has served as guest editor for several publications. Hansel leads writing workshops and retreats virtually and in the Greater Cincinnati area and beyond. Visit her website at https://paulettahansel.wordpress.com/.

www.ingramcontent.com/pod-product-compliance
Lightning Source LLC
Chambersburg PA
CBHW020443090526
44586CB00045B/824